WITHDRAWN

How to Live with a
Problem Drinker
AND SURVIVE

How to Live with a
Problem Drinker
AND SURVIVE

GARY G. FORREST, Ed.D., P.C.

EXECUTIVE DIRECTOR, PSYCHOTHERAPY
ASSOCIATES, P.C. AND THE INSTITUTE FOR
ADDICTIVE BEHAVIORAL CHANGE, COLORADO
SPRINGS, COLORADO

C. 1

NEW YORK   1980   *Atheneum*

Library of Congress Cataloging in Publication Data

Forrest, Gary G
    How to live with a problem drinker and survive.

    1.   Alcoholics—Family relationships.   I.   Title.
HV5132.F67   1980   362.8'2   79-55620
ISBN   0-689-11038-3

Published simultaneously in Canada by McClelland
and Stewart Ltd.
Manufactured by Fairfield Graphics, Fairfield, Pennsylvania
Designed by Kathleen Carey
First Edition

To Sandra and Sarah Ellen

Foreword

One of the greatest influences in my life was our family doctor. His name was Dr. Charles Coughlin, but to all seven of us kids—each one of whom he delivered in our house on Powers Street in Baltimore—he was known as "Uncle Doc."

You can't define charisma; you simply sense it or experience it. Whatever it is, Uncle Doc had it. When he walked into the house, we all knew instinctively that everything was going to be all right. He was the kind of man who made things better.

Like Uncle Doc, Gary Forrest is a man who makes things better. In his private practice and in his work with other practitioners, he has demonstrated time and again the effectiveness of his approach in confronting and solving the problem of alcoholism. At the root of his success, I think, is compassion. A nonalcoholic himself, he has gone out of his way to become familiar with the mind and heart of the alcoholic, and with the pain that this so-called family disease inflicts on everyone involved. All of his techniques for helping problem drinkers and their families derive from an intimate and humane understanding of the plight of others. Dr. Forrest writes directly, with warmth and sincerity, and without jargon, and his book will be enormously comforting and useful to any person trapped in an intimate relationship with a problem drinker.

Father Joseph C. Martin
Havre de Grace, Maryland
January 1980

Contents

How to Live with a
Problem Drinker

AND SURVIVE

Don't Let Someone Else's Drinking Problem Destroy YOUR Life

Is there a problem drinker in your life?

It is likely that there is, or you would not have opened this book. Let me go one step further. If you *suspect* that a loved one has a drinking problem, then I am willing to bet you that person is psychologically and/or physiologically dependent on the chemical substance ethyl alcohol, and that you and your relationship with that person are suffering as a result.

Doctors and social scientists disagree on a precise definition of alcoholism. But let's be practical. From my experience in working almost exclusively with problem drinkers and their families over the past ten years, I can assure you that if you are worried or otherwise adversely affected by the drinking behavior of someone you love, whether it be spouse, parent or child, then it is in your best interest to act on the assumption that your loved one is indeed an alcoholic. (Since clinical distinctions between "alcoholic" and "problem drinker" are of no immediate concern to the vast majority, the terms have been used interchangeably throughout the book.)

This book is written primarily for people who are living with a person with a drinking problem. Spouses of problem drinkers head the list of those most affected by the pathological drinking patterns of others. It is also no easy task for children to live with a parent who has a drinking problem, and they are often physically and emotionally crippled as a result. Today in America, many adolescents and preteens have serious drinking problems, so parents may also benefit by reading this book. Millions of employers, business partners and members of the work force must deal on a daily basis with a colleague or associate with a drinking problem; their plight is also considered.

Finally, many people have a friend, neighbor or roommate with a drinking problem, and they, too, need to be better prepared to be of real help.

From this proceeds our main purpose—to help you survive this most destructive of human relationships. For if you are living with an alcoholic, you are now more involved in the process of dying than in the rich experience of life. You owe it to yourself—and, ultimately, to the person with the drinking problem—to face this reality.

You are certainly not alone in this problem. There are presently ten to eleven million alcoholics in the United States. More than half of these addicted individuals are married and have children. Over eighty percent of them are also employed. It has been estimated that every person with a serious drinking problem affects the emotional health and well-being of five other people. Conservatively, then, we can say at least forty-five to fifty million Americans today either have a drinking problem, or are adversely and variously affected by a problem drinker.

If it is true that you are living with a problem drinker, you may sense that you are in a kind of trap in your life. The problem drinker is, in essence, trapped in a bottle, and you are trapped in this same bottle. The spouse, children and loved ones of any problem drinker are in the bottle together. All become emotionally upset and confused, and experience social and financial problems as a result of the many difficulties of the problem drinker. The trap is a diffuse and all-encompassing reality. The trap is also cancerous in that the conflicts of the problem drinker eventually spread and include everyone in the family as well as friends and fellow workers.

For all that, it is possible for victims of an alcoholic relationship to escape from this trap, if they begin to work at living differently in ways I will describe shortly. Indeed, unless you are fatalistically prepared to accept your own premature psychological and even physical death, it is vital that you understand the nature of the alcoholic relationship and make changes that will set you free from its many dangers.

This book contains guidelines and strategies that have helped others grow and behave rationally and responsibly in spite of the presence of a loved one who is a problem drinker. These guidelines can help you too, if you are willing to make a commitment to changing yourself and your relationship, and to put in the time and effort this process will involve. It may be cold comfort, but bear in mind that you are already

putting in much time and work, probably un-
productively, to survive in your present situation. Why not devote the same amount of energy
toward building a healthier, happier life for
yourself?

Trademarks of a Serious Drinking Problem

Let's look more closely at what constitutes problem drinking, so that you can be more certain in your own mind about whether or not you are living with a problem drinker.

First, I'll define four specific traits of drinking behavior common to problem drinkers. Then I will sketch in some of the more general characteristics of the personality and emotional life of the problem drinker. These are the things that color your present relationship with your loved one on a day-to-day basis, and probably determine virtually all your major conflicts and difficulties with that person. By becoming more familiar with both the drinking pattern and overall persona of the problem drinker, you will be in a much better position to take the next step—to begin to extricate yourself from the clutches of the problem.

Approximately twenty-five percent of the American adult population are nondrinkers. Most people who do drink are not problem drinkers but social drinkers—people who consume two or three alcoholic beverages on one or two occasions per week, or less. They may get drunk three or four times a year, but they are still social drinkers without a real alcohol problem.

Here are the four traits that distinguish the problem drinker from the social drinker.

1. *The problem drinker drinks compulsively, and can't really control such factors as when, where and how much he or she drinks.* Most alcoholics will vehemently deny that they can't control their urge to drink. Problem drinkers may "cut down," or "go on the wagon" to convince others, as well as themselves, that they can handle the drinking. By quitting for a few days, weeks or even months, problem drinkers frequently feel they have proven that they are

not alcoholics. They also may switch brands of their usual alcoholic beverage, or change from Scotch to vodka, or from vodka to bourbon, all in an effort to establish some semblance of control over their addiction. They may announce their decision to drink "only" beer, the inference being that beer drinkers can't be alcoholics. In fact, any beverage with alcohol in it can be abused to the point of addiction.

The compulsive nature of the disorder has been well established, but it is extremely hard for the social drinker or nondrinker to fully comprehend it. Think back to the last time you had a bad toothache or earache. Your near constant awareness of that throbbing pain during that time would be quite similar to the obsessive interest in drink experienced by an alcoholic.

2. *The problem drinker has been drinking for many years.* Some people, more typically women, can become addicted to alcohol in a short period of time—within two or three years or even in a matter of months. In such cases, the death of a child, parent or spouse is often clearly associated with the precipitous decline into alcoholism. But generally, and particularly as regards male drinkers, the process of addiction occurs over a long period of time.

3. *The problem drinker drinks to the point of*

intoxication. It may not always be readily apparent, but anyone who consumes four or five alcoholic drinks of any kind within an hour or two is intoxicated. Many problem drinkers, particularly in the earlier stages of their addiction, are able to mask the symptoms generally associated with drunkenness. In most cases, the addiction does not prevent an alcoholic from performing most of his or her duties. Indeed, some seventy-five to eighty percent of the persons who have been identified as alcoholics in this country are members of the work force, including many with successful professional careers. Popular opinion formerly visualized the typical alcoholic as the "skid row" variety, but in fact the grossly dysfunctional, chronically unemployed drinker comprises less than five percent of the alcoholic population. In recent years, many celebrities and political figures have openly acknowledged their personal struggles with drinking. This has made the American public more aware of the fact that alcoholism is socioeconomically widespread.

It should be noted here that in advanced stages of alcoholism, the amount a person can consume without showing signs of intoxication drops sharply. In the case of a chronic alcoholic entering the final stages of the addiction process, three or four drinks may bring on the kind of behavior that required a pint or fifth to precipitate a year earlier.

4. *The drinking activity of a problem drinker produces severe problems in the important relationships in his or her life.* Problem drinkers invariably have people problems. If they are married, their marriages are full of conflict. Very often they also have conflicts with other relatives, employers, fellow workers and neighbors. "I can't get along with anyone, myself included," is a refrain I hear frequently from the problem drinkers I work with. A major reason many alcoholics begin to drink heavily is to feel comfortable in their relationships with other people. Yet, as a result of the drinking, they lose real contact with loved ones and close friends and associates. They progressively remove themselves from the realm of healthy human relationships into a world characterized by isolation, detachment and loneliness.

A distinction should be made here between physiological and psychological addiction to alcohol. From your own point of view, the effect of living with a problem drinker may be just the same in either case. But it is important to understand the difference in the consequences to the individual of the two conditions.

Persons who are physiologically addicted must continuously ingest alcohol in order to deter bodily or physiological withdrawal symptoms. When the physically addicted alcoholic quits drinking, he or she experiences acute anxiety, agitation, possibly hallucinations and delusions, disorganization and changes in pulse, respiration, coordination, motor skills, blood pressure and the other basic vital signs. Such drastic body systems changes are clinically referred to as delirium tremens and are commonly called the DTs or "the shakes." Every chronic alcoholic who has attempted to quit drinking on his or her own (going "cold turkey") has experienced this syndrome to a varying extent. The chronic alcoholic is well aware of the terror brought about by discontinuing the drinking process, which is why he or she will go to great lengths to be assured of another drink. Such an alcoholic is notoriously shaky upon rising in the morning because a borderline alcohol withdrawal process has taken place during sleep. That's why the physically addicted individual *must* have a drink after awakening— to nullify the withdrawal symptoms.

Psychological addiction means a dependence upon alcohol short of a bodily and physiological need. Persons who are psychologically addicted to alcohol typically feel they must have two or three cocktails every night. These people may deny an actual craving for the regular two or three drinks, but their behavior conveys a different message. Psychological addiction often takes the form of "binge drinking" or the "weekend drunk" syndrome. This is one definite form of problem drinking. Some of my patients reported they would begin to drink immediately following work on a Friday afternoon and continue drinking until late Sunday night. Others abstained completely from drinking for weeks or months before ending up drunk and in trouble again.

Many chronic alcoholics develop cirrhosis of the liver, gastrointestinal complications, kidney damage, malnutrition and neurological impairments. Commonly, these medical conditions result in a yellowing or jaundiced skin appearance, reddening of the eyes, ulcers or borderline ulcerative and digestive problems, urinary pain and complications, physical weakness and chronic fatigue, poor or impaired memory, confusion and emotional problems. The person who is psychologically dependent upon alcohol rarely suffers these extreme ills. But if the psychological addict does develop physical dependence, as happens in roughly sixty percent of the cases, he or she also becomes exposed to these severe side effects. From my observation, this escalation into physiological addiction usually occurs when the persistent problem drinker reaches forty-five or fifty years of age.

Traits of the Problem Drinker

Now let's focus on some of the more personal behavioral traits of the person who has trouble with alcohol. Problem drinkers are individual human beings and necessarily differ from each other in myriad ways. At the same time, we have discovered from observation and through counseling that they are alike in many ways as well. There are things almost universally true about the personality makeup, emotional life and style of relating to other people of virtually all alcoholics. As I mentioned, these are the things that probably dominate your present relationship and cause you the most heartache and despair if, in fact, your loved one is a problem drinker.

You will probably recognize him or her in the pages which follow. In order to evaluate the problem drinker honestly and objectively, you must detach yourself emotionally from that person. Attempt to evaluate him or her from the perspective you might take in meeting a stranger for the first time at a social gathering. What do you see? If you recognize any of the traits that follow and can begin to accept the reality of the drinker's personality and behavior, you will be better equipped to initiate self and relationship changes which may also help the problem drinker change constructively.

THEY ARE ANXIOUS.

If your loved one is a problem drinker, he or she is a chronically anxious person. Problem drinkers attempt to use alcohol as an anti-anxiety agent. Anxiety shows up in physical hyperactivity, restlessness and a perpetual sense of uneasiness. The problem drinker is anxious and uncomfortable particularly in his or her relationships with other people. Many alcoholics have told me, "I can't sit still," "I'm always on the go," "I'm a bundle of nerves," and other variations on the same theme. Irrational fears contribute to the sense of being anxious. A problem drinker has many of these irrational fears, although he or she may attempt in many ways to convince you and others that "fear" is not in his or her vocabulary. Sleep disturbance is common to the chronic alcoholic: anxious dreams or nightmares, waking in the middle of the night, shaking and sweating. The alcoholic drinks in order to relieve anxiety, but during even the early stages of the addiction process, heavy drinking causes acute anxiety.

THEY ARE ANGRY.

If you are living with a problem drinker, chances are that he or she is frequently angry at you, any children you may have and, indeed, the entire world. Alcoholism is a disorder of rage. Passive, dependent and seemingly nonangry problem drinkers direct their rage at themselves—and frequently destroy themselves in the process. Overtly aggressive alcoholics tend to direct these feelings and behaviors against those closest to them; in other words, *against you*. The problem drinker usually radiates his or her anger and violence onto other people and onto the environment. But he or she is adept at arranging things so that the result of the rage does not appear to be the drinker's fault.

Does the problem drinker in your life tend to blame you for his inappropriate anger and hostility? Do you get a "you made me do it" message from him in the wake of some verbal outburst or physical act of destruction? People close to alcoholics fall for this "setup" hundreds of times—and feel guilty every time. It is not uncommon for a problem drinker to wreck cars, physically abuse his or her spouse and children, or physically hurt and even destroy his or her own person. Another favorite, if less dramatic, channel for the alcoholic's rage is verbal abuse. Many problem drinkers may never hit their loved ones, but will use words to assault them.

THEY ARE MANIPULATIVE.

If you are living with a problem drinker, you have probably felt manipulated and used by him or her on hundreds of occasions. The alcoholic is a con artist and can be extremely adept at getting others to do what he or she wants them to do. The spouse of the problem drinker can relate to the following situations. Have you noticed that *you* are always the one to face the bill collectors? Do *you* frequently end up calling the boss or supervisor to let him or her know that your alcoholic won't be able to come to work today because he or she is sick or has the flu? Are *you* the one who goes to the school when a child has gotten in trouble?

These are but a few of the areas in which the alcoholic arranges, through manipulation, for a loved one to cover up or otherwise be responsible for his or her irresponsible behavior. Problem drinkers "con" their way in and out of situations which many of us would never dream of attempting. The problem drinker often has an uncanny awareness of the weaknesses and strengths of other people and uses this ability to his or her advantage at the expense of others.

THEY ARE TYRANNICAL.

The problem drinker is completely out of control with regard to his or her drinking, as mentioned earlier. Yet, paradoxically, your problem drinker probably controls you. In part, this is because you have let your thoughts and feelings be manipulated by that person. The problem drinker cries, begs, pleads and promises "never to do it again" in order to control you, and may have been successful hundreds of times in such endeavors. In addition, problem drinkers naturally tend to act like dictators and tyrants, especially at home and with loved ones. The problem drinker neurotically tries to control his or her world in order to somehow feel in control of self. Problem drinkers are afraid of life and terrified about dying, the ultimate loss of control. Related to these matters, the problem drinker is morbidly afraid of "losing his mind" or "going crazy."

THEY ARE SELF-DELUDING.

Every problem drinker denies that he or she is addicted to alcohol. Beyond this basic self-deception, problem drinkers tend to deny most reality-oriented issues, especially when they are personally threatening or create feelings of discomfort. Your drinker will stubbornly avoid discussing uneasy feelings or taking steps to change problematical situations, and will deny they are problems for either of you. Through intoxication, the drinker creates a distorted world free of the real problems of existence.

THEY ARE DEPENDENT.

We are all dependent beings from the time of conception until we die, but the problem drinker is overly dependent in many areas of living. If your drinker is your husband, I suspect that you have frequently felt more like a mother than a wife in your relationship.

Dependency conflicts are usually expressed in oral ways. Thus the typical heavy drinker is also a heavy smoker. When and if the alcoholic quits drinking, he or she usually begins to eat more and puts on weight, continues to smoke heavily and drinks cup after cup of coffee or some other beverage.

Most drinkers have struggled for years with dependency needs. But as masters in denial, they tend to cover up these needs. Male alcoholics often engage in various behaviors to convince you and others of their "supermasculinity." Playing the role of tough guy or

Mr. Big, using foul language and womanizing are some of the maneuvers he employs to convince others of his self-sufficiency and independence.

THEY ARE DEPRESSED.

Every problem drinker I have ever worked with had a longstanding struggle with feelings of depression. Some alcoholics avoid a conscious awareness of depression by acting-out. This is a psychological term for the process of resolving internal conflicts and problems by external means. Rather than attempting to resolve depression internally, the problem drinker often turns to alcohol, other drugs or sexual promiscuity as solutions.

Feeling "down in the dumps," dwelling upon the past and blaming or pitying oneself are modes indicative of a drinker's depressive struggles. Feelings of inadequacy, inferiority and worthlessness underlie and create depression.

Some drinkers appear to be on an emotional roller coaster—"up" one day, "down" the next. Psychiatrists and clinical psychologists often misdiagnose the chronic alcoholic with such mood changes as a manic-depressive. Even the "up" mood swings of the problem drinker can be viewed as a means of avoiding depression. Rather commonly, alcoholics become very depressed after they quit drinking. Recovery dictates dealing internally with depression, something they have consciously striven to avoid, via alcohol, in the past.

THEY ARE IRRESPONSIBLE.

Irresponsibility in this context means *not* telling the truth, *not* following through on commitments and obligations, *not* paying bills on time or refusing to pay them, period, and *not* being honest. Your problem drinker does what he or she wants, when he or she wants to do it, and usually without consulting you. Self-centeredness or egocentricity is at the heart of the drinker's irresponsible behavior. As a loved one, your biggest problem with this trait probably has been your attempt to assume responsibility for his or her irresponsibility. As a result, you may have taught your drinker that he or she really doesn't need to behave responsibly, because you will take care of these matters.

THEY ARE IMMATURE.

The problem drinker behaves and interacts with loved ones and others in ways not appropriate to his or her age. Sulking, temper tantrums and impulsive or irresponsible behavior demonstrate that the "adult" alcoholic is an immature individual. One of the basic effects of a severe drinking problem is an arrest in personality development. The alcoholic ages in a chronological sense, but he or she fails to grow and mature emotionally and psychologically once the addiction process begins. In fact, the alcoholic regresses as the addiction progresses. Your problem drinker will become more childish and adolescentlike the more dependent upon alcohol he or she becomes. Some of the alcoholics I have successfully worked with told me they had to "grow up all over again" once they terminated their addiction. One patient said that, in spite of being fifty years old, he had "behaved, thought and felt" like a fourteen-year-old until he broke his alcohol dependency.

Adolescent problem drinkers lose, in part, the ability to grow psychologically, mature and become fully functioning as a result of their early developed pattern of problem drinking.

THEY NURTURE INFERIORITY/ GRANDIOSITY FEELINGS.

Very often the problem drinker feels a deep sense of inferiority, inadequacy and worthlessness. He or she is keenly in touch with these feelings and is disgusted all the more as a result. Many alcoholics have, in fact, been "losers" for most of their lives. Dropping out of school, losing jobs, failing in relationships with parents and other friends and loved ones, all contribute mightily to the failure identity of an alcoholic. Many such drinkers first experience a sense of inferiority and inadequacy in childhood, and have grown up with a self-concept devoid of positive perceptions.

In an attempt to reject his or her personal sense of worthlessness, your drinker may be a grandiose, self-centered type of person who is driven by needs for personal power and omnipotence. Buying a "round for the bar," telling you how "damned stupid" you are, and spending money extravagantly are some methods alcoholics use to convey their superiority. Everyone *but* the drinker usually recognizes that feelings of inadequacy underlie such behavior.

THEY ARE IMPATIENT.

Problem drinkers are impulsive people with a low tolerance for frustration or stress. They are short-tempered, quick to fly off the handle. Instead of trying to cope with life rationally, they become angry, agitated and tense. Their means of coping with the frustrations of daily living is drinking. If the 5:35 P.M. commuter train is fifteen minutes late, the problem drinker may swallow two double martinis while waiting rather than deal with the time in a more adaptive and constructive manner, such as reading a book or pursuing business on the phone.

Problem drinkers never view themselves as being the source of low frustration tolerance. It is always others who put them out, who make them wait, who frustrate them. They cannot abide even moderate levels of stress without reacting nervously.

Low frustration tolerance relates to the tendency of many problem drinkers to drink heavily when they fly on airplanes. The stress of flying, fear of losing control, and similar factors contribute to the pattern of having three or four drinks prior to getting on the airplane and then drinking more once in flight.

THEY HAVE SEXUAL PROBLEMS.

Many alcoholics have sexual problems which significantly affect their lives. These problems include impotence, frigidity, premature ejaculation and promiscuity. Some problem drinkers are totally uninterested in sex, with spouses or anyone else. Others conduct one illicit affair after another. The exact nature of the sexual problem is unique to the individual. Often it is the sexual problem that causes the person with the drinking problem to enter therapy. A man with long-term problem drinking behavior came to me mainly because he had not engaged in any form of sexual activity with his wife for nearly ten years. He was extremely wealthy, intelligent and only forty-eight years old, but he believed he was "over the hill" sexually. Another patient and his wife entered therapy due to retarded ejaculation. After drinking heavily, the couple engaged in a wide variety of sexual acts for hours at a time, but the patient was unable to ejaculate. One married alcoholic woman entered therapy after a binge during which she contracted venereal disease.

Commonly, sexual conflicts in problem drinkers are closely associated with the matter of identity. The alcoholic drinks in order to be somebody. More specifically, many alcoholics drink in order to be a "man" or a "woman." Alcoholic males who behave promiscuously are trying to prove to themselves and to others that they are, in fact, masculine. Women alcoholics drink in part to demonstrate their warmth and femininity. The alcoholic has never fully resolved the question, "Who am I?" Uncertainty with regard to one's sexual identity can produce any number of psychological symptoms, and alcoholism is one of them.

A proclivity toward the traits and behavior discussed in this chapter exists in the problem drinker even prior to the onset of symptomatic drinking. With drinking and intoxication, the problem drinker becomes more depressed, anxious, angry, impulsive, manipulative and self-centered. In other words, the drinking itself accentuates the basic personality and behavioral problems. Problem drinking is a progressive disorder. As your problem drinker drinks more, he or she will display more of these traits. As he or she develops more pathological patterns of alcohol consumption, he or she loses the ability to conceal these traits.

While there is no one alcoholic personality, the combination of personality and behavioral traits discussed in this chapter constitutes a framework which includes the personality structure and life-style of the problem drinker. The problem drinker thinks, feels, behaves within this framework and can be identified according to these traits.

Traits of the Person Living with a Problem Drinker

If your relationship with a loved one suffers to any degree as a result of the drinking behavior of that person as just described, you can be sure that *both* of you have an alcohol-related problem. You may not be living with a chronic alcoholic, but the difficulties which arise as a result of his or her drinking behavior also have involved you in a destructive process which needs to be confronted and changed.

Here are the six most common behavioral traits that I have observed in the lives of people living with problem drinkers, presented in the order in which they tend to surface in the course of the relationship.

THEY DENY THE TRUTH.

Anyone caught in a relationship with a problem drinker eventually begins to exhibit certain of the self-defeating traits of that person. At the top of this list, we find the trait of denial.

Naturally, people prefer not to admit they might be living with an alcoholic, so denial comes easily in the early stages of such a relationship. The loved one might be a "heavy drinker," "drunk," "Scotch lover," an "occasional boozer," or someone who "likes to have a good time," but he or she certainly is not an alcoholic.

Friends and loved ones become part of the crazy drinking behavior as a way of avoiding the reality of the problem. Bowing to the suggestion from the problem drinker that things will be better between them if they would just "party together," they get drunk with the person. Indeed, the alcoholic will make his or her companion feel guilty for not "letting go" or "having a ball,"—meaning, drinking together.

Accomplice-like, friends and loved ones often

spend a good deal of time and energy covering up for the drinker's problem. Making excuses to employers, co-workers, other family members, friends and relatives for misbehavior is basic to this insidious pattern of denial.

THEY "ACT-OUT" THE PROBLEM.

As indicated earlier, acting-out is a psychological term for the impulsive, immature and sometimes grossly irresponsible behavior that a person engages in to cope with internal emotional stress.

Most friends and loved ones of serious problem drinkers eventually resort to acting-out in one form or another. Drinking with the problem drinker is actually a primitive kind of acting-out. At later stages, the latent hostility brought on by the conflict begins to express itself in more clearly negative activity, such as shouting matches (not necessarily centered on drinking) and even physical assaults.

Geographical moves and extramarital affairs are more dramatic forms of acting-out.

Youngsters in the shadow of a parent's drinking problem frequently translate their emotional difficulties into poor school performance, sexual promiscuity, drug and/or alcohol abuse, lying, fighting and stealing. In such conduct they are expressing the anger and resentment they feel at being caught in the problem drinker's trap.

THEY BECOME REFORMERS.

Most people who live with a problem drinker eventually try to change or reform their problem drinker. They may choose to fight this battle for months, years or even for a lifetime, in the belief that "everything will be all right if only I can stop his [or her] drinking." Unfortunately, this invariably results in a losing battle for all concerned. The more one works at changing the problem drinker, the more the problem drinker resists the attempts. The problem drinker becomes enraged by "preaching" or "nagging" and usually decides to imbibe even more. The loved one becomes increasingly frustrated and disturbed as the futile effort continues.

THEY BECOME ISOLATED.

People who live with an alcoholic eventually find themselves virtually alone in the world. Though it may go unnoticed for years, a process of estrangement from friends, family and community sets in within months of the onset of a severe drinking problem in a relationship. As the drinker's problem intensifies, the loved one instinctively reduces frequency of contact with neighbors and relatives. If an alcoholic man accuses his wife of having an affair with the preacher, naturally the wife is inclined to stay away from church. If an alcoholic woman speaks incoherently to her children in the afternoon, naturally the children will be disinclined to bring home friends after school.

The spouse of an alcoholic usually suffers more from loneliness than the alcoholic does. The drinker may become progressively more isolated, but booze blocks some of the lonely feelings intrinsic to his or her condition. Also, the alcoholic usually has friendships with people such as drinking cohorts, bartenders or work associates. These are limited relationships at best, but they serve to somewhat mask the drinker's solitary condition.

Generally, children of problem drinkers are

able to find and sustain a few meaningful peer relationships and so keep at least one foot in the real world. Not so for the spouse who is "cooperating" with a serious problem drinker.

THEY GIVE UP.

After a number of years of living with a drinking alcoholic (in contrast to living with a sober alcoholic who is actually involved in therapy or AA) most people are reduced to a level of chronic neurotic depression. They roll with their drinker's punches, both literally and figuratively. There is no end to the tunnel they are in. Life has become a constant burden with few, if any, moments of genuine pleasure or fun. Complaints and negative attitudes dominate the mind. Lethargy, discomfort, various physical complaints and chronic fatigue become the bodily expressions of this process. Many women who live with an alcoholic become overweight— for them, food is the vehicle by which they can experience the closest thing to love left to them in life.

THEY GO CRAZY.

By "going crazy" I mean that most people who accept living with a problem drinker on the drinker's terms eventually exhibit any of a wide variety of severe psychological and physical ills, including the most extreme form, outright madness.

Some of the physical ills brought on by the years of being trapped within a deeply disturbed alcoholic relationship are ulcers, backaches, migraine headaches, stomach problems, radical weight gain or loss, severe anxiety attacks, chronic fatigue and insomnia.

Suicide or confinement to psychiatric wards are also common fates.

Traits of a Loving Relationship

There are different ways of looking at the problem of living with an alcoholic. The simple word "living" can mean many different things to different people. Personally, I believe living with a drinking alcoholic is less than living. If you have been doing so, my guess is that you have deprived yourself of many of the most rewarding and enjoyable aspects of human existence. If your problem drinker beats you every night, then surely life is wretched for you. But even if your alcoholic is not generally angry, hostile or physically abusive, I feel sure you are still giving up a lot by choosing to live with that person.

Recall for a moment the good things that are possible in a relationship between two persons living together on intimate terms. Let me share with you my thoughts on the optimal conditions for such a relationship and ask you to compare these conditions with the ones that exist in your particular relationship with a problem drinker. These optimal conditions apply to all varieties of intimate human relationships—marital, familial and friendship—which are healthy and growth-oriented to the extent that they are based upon the conditions.

After considering this information, I hope you will be ready and willing to make the decisions and changes that will be necessary in order for you to get on with your life in a more rewarding and fulfilling fashion.

MUTUAL CONCERN.

A sense of *mutual* concern and respect are essential ingredients in any healthy human relationship. When two or more human beings base a relationship on reciprocal concern, all parties involved are able to feel *personally* valued and secure. Such relationships necessitate a capacity to love oneself and others, to express love in mutually understandable ways, to interact in ways which enhance and promote the general well-being of each person. It may sound strange, but the capacity to love and be concerned about others begins with the ability to love and like oneself. When we are unable to love ourselves we are unable to love others.

Seemingly unimportant transactions are very much a part of this process—little things do mean a lot. Telling your loved one that he or she "looks nice today," that you appreciate something he or she has done for you, that you enjoy that person's company, conversation or cuisine are significant gestures in any healthy relationship.

When only one person is able to be concerned, loving and giving, the relationship becomes by definition one-sided. Adaptive human living is not parasitic in nature.

Is there a consistent sense of mutual concern, giving and loving in your relationship with the problem drinker?

JOINT GROWTH.

Perpetual *change* and *growth* are marks of a healthy, dynamic relationship. Static relationships are seldom rewarding for long. We begin to become unhappy, unproductive and dissatisfied with ourselves and others when we stop learning, growing and changing. As individuals we need to continuously grow and change. So, too, in our most important relationships, we must see positive development; otherwise relationships become stale and moribund.

Are you and your problem drinker changing and growing in mutually beneficial ways?

AUTONOMY FOR EACH.

There is a need for autonomy and individuality in addition to mutuality and dependence in any intimate relationship. Healthy coexistence involves a great deal of mutual giving and working and playing together, but this process becomes unhealthy or disturbed when one of the people involved is unable to maintain a strong sense of individuality *within* the context of the relationship. If there is a basic lack of independence and separateness, the person will soon experience a sense of powerlessness and inadequacy. As we grow and change in our relationships, we must also grow and change as individuals in these relationships. All of us must maintain our separate identities in order to live fully.

Many people believe that successful marriages, families and friendships are based upon doing things together, having the same feelings and sharing the same perceptions, beliefs, attitudes and values. Nothing could be further from the truth. Healthy and adaptive human relationships always provide for individuality. We must be able to allow the people we are most intimately involved with the opportunity to maintain their own feelings and beliefs. Whenever one person in an intimate relationship attempts, consciously or unconsciously, to shape or determine the attitudes and values of another person or other persons involved in the relationship, the relationship suffers. Ultimately, we must be able to take the risk of helping our loved ones develop their individuality to the fullest.

Has your identity been strengthened or diminished by the relationship you have with a problem drinker?

Loving Relationship

"NO-FAULT" COMMUNICATION.

A fourth requirement for healthy loving relationships is that of being *consistently uncritical* of the person or persons we are living with.

We live in a highly judgmental atmosphere in today's world. We get critical evaluations on the job, through casual contacts and through the media. These "critiques" can directly affect and shape our self-concept, for better or worse. The last thing we need from those who supposedly love and cherish us is the put-down or the sarcastic remark. In a positive, fruitful relationship, people talk in encouraging, supportive, positive terms. Rancor or fault-finding is practically nonexistent. There is a sympathetic attitude toward one another's problems and fears. Within the context of positive, "no-fault" communication, there must always be a consistent amount of constructive criticism and feedback. Constructive criticism is not communicated as a "put-down."

Does the problem drinker in your life refrain from faultfinding, petty criticism and resentful confrontation?

SHARING.

Healthy and happy relationships are built around sharing experiences. Couples, families and friendships depend on them. Going out for dinner or on a family picnic engages the deep needs for ordinary sharing in all of us. When we terminate such activities we begin to lose our mutual sense of involvement, commonality and contact.

Healthy relationships include emotional, intellectual and experiential sharing. Effective communication is essential to all of these forms of sharing. Sharing feelings and emotions can be threatening and difficult, yet people who are involved in meaningful relationships are consistently able to share and talk about their feelings with each other. They are able to share their moment-to-moment daily life experiences. They live life together, as a unit as well as individuals sharing the experience of life.

Is there a good deal of consistent sharing in your relationship with the problem drinker?

SUCCOR FOR EACH.

When we are able to live with another human being in the context of a healthy and loving relationship, we have the chance to play an important role in helping that other person become whatever he or she is capable of becoming. Optimal psychological development becomes possible through optimal healthy interpersonal relationships. When we help others develop, grow and become fully functioning, we have a profound impact upon their self-concept and self-esteem. We can actually influence the personality and feelings of the people we are living with in a positive, creative way.

Helping a spouse, child or friend actualize his or her potential for living can be a source of joy and reward. But in order to accomplish this task, we must be able to put aside our own insecurities, jealousies and fears. Creative living demands a great deal. If one is unhappy in major interpersonal relationships, it is nearly impossible to help others in their attempts to live creatively.

Does your problem drinker help you in your struggle to become whatever it is in life that you can or want to become?

HAVING FUN.

Finally, all healthy human relationships include having fun. If we are going to live with a spouse or friend or family member for an extended period of time, we must be able to experience some fun doing it. Most of us tend to underestimate the importance of fun in our lives. We are so caught up in work, getting ahead and "surviving" that we forget our needs and opportunities for fun. Many of us lose the ability to have fun. But the longer we live with others, the more important it becomes to experience enjoyment, humor and fun *with* the people we love. We need to be able to *play* with those we are living with. Life is not limited to work, drudgery and routine. Taking vacations and enjoying recreational activities are familiar but often neglected forms of fun. Having fun also includes the ability to experience the many amusing vagaries of life with others. People who live together adaptively join in smiling and laughing at things.

Is your alcoholic fun to be around?

Living successfully and optimally with another human being involves more than the seven conditions I have just mentioned. Understanding and defining roles, setting rules, understanding power and control issues, and hundreds of other items also relate to effective or ineffective human contacts, and all these have been examined at length by behavioral scientists. Still, when we study the divergent viewpoints regarding "what it takes" to be able to live successfully with another person or persons, the seven conditions I have discussed are the most fundamental. These are the ones you should find consistently satisfied, at least to some degree, in your most important relationships.

After assessing your style of living with a problem drinker, you are likely to feel depressed, cheated and angry. Don't let these feelings give you the idea that you have nothing to live for or look forward to. You have it within your power to change that afflicted relationship and to begin to survive in more rewarding and meaningful ways—with, without or in spite of the problem drinker! The rest of this book is directed toward helping you accomplish this task.

Steps Toward
Changing Yourself

It is difficult, if not impossible, to significantly change the problem drinking behavior or general behavior and life-style of those closest to you. Whether the problem drinker in your life is a parent, spouse, child or close friend, you cannot "make" that person "not be" an alcoholic. Even psychologists and psychiatrists have learned that it is hard work to help their patients change. Most now agree that in the end it is the patient who is most responsible for changing himself or herself. From my own psychotherapy practice I have observed that when a person tries to change the behavior of someone else, new difficulties arise in the relationship. The harder one works at forcing another person to change, the greater the degree and variety of problems that ensue. People find themselves being confronted with new conflicts as a result of their reformist zeal. The person who is being pressured to change also experiences new and different difficulties as a result. I do feel that each of us can make it *easier* for another person to choose to alter or change his or her behavior. But we can't make that choice for the person.

The only person any of us can ever really hope to change is ourself. If change does occur, relationships with other people inevitably change as well.

All of us are afraid of change to varying degrees. Indeed, most people work very hard at *not* changing because to do so would involve risk. Changing means experiencing something new, different and unknown. Even if your relationship with a problem drinker has been akin to "living in a garbage pail" for many years, you may be quite reluctant to take the risks involved in changing yourself within this relationship. Typically, the alcoholic and his or her loved ones strive to maintain a sense of sameness and predictability in their relationship. Review your own troubled relationship for a moment and see if it is not true that you have had the same arguments, fights, enjoyments, struggles and life experiences with your problem drinker for most of the duration of that relationship.

The most unfortunate thing about the change-resistant pattern you are caught in may be that you dislike or plain hate what you're doing. Certainly, you dislike the alcohol-facilitated behavior of your problem drinker. In addition, you probably dislike yourself for being so stuck, for being in such a bind, for letting your life slip beyond your power to alter or control.

If you accept the premise that the only person in your troubled relationship that you can change is yourself, and if you are willing to make the commitment to changing, you are capable of radically turning things around in your life. The following six steps are fundamental to the process of freeing yourself from the self-defeating aspects of living with a problem drinker.

1. *Stop taking responsibility for the actions of your problem drinker.* This may sound harsh and selfish, and in a way it is. But as long as you assume responsibility for the misbehaviors of

your problem drinker, he or she will continue to behave as always. As long as you make it easy for the problem drinker to drink irresponsibly by covering up or by doing the things he or she should be doing, you will not begin to grow and change as you want to. Obviously, you cannot shirk your responsibility as a parent, in the case of young children. It is the irresponsible behaviors of the problem drinker that you must begin to leave be. This means that if your problem drinker is unable to go to work, he or she should call the boss or employer—*not you!* If your problem drinker refuses to do vital chores such as paying a bill on time or having the car repaired, let him or her suffer from the consequences, *not you.* In this context, you must be responsible for yourself. Suggest to the bill-collector that he contact the problem drinker at work. If *your* car needs to be repaired, see to it that it gets fixed! Don't make yourself upset by waiting for the problem drinker to take your car to the garage for repairs. If he or she phones you in a state of intoxication from a bar, don't give in to the impulse to go out and bring that person home safely. And don't remain awake and worried until that person finally arrives home. You are not responsible for the problem drinker. You cannot control how he or she gets home. Your worrying will accomplish absolutely nothing.

When you assume responsibility for your problem drinker, you actually reinforce his or her drinking behavior. You become a "permitter." Eventually, you will make yourself increasingly angry and upset for making it easier for this person to drink.

2. *Stop taking physical or verbal abuse from your problem drinker.* Your problem drinker probably has been denigrating you in many ways for a long time. It is time for you to stop serving as that person's punching bag, literally or figuratively. Allowing yourself to be abused contributes heavily to your feeling upset and lacking a personal sense of strength, dignity and self-respect.

Verbal warnings rarely suffice to stop the physically abusive alcoholic, particularly while that person is drinking. In fact, such warnings may result in even more physical violence directed against you. Instead, you must inform the alcoholic over and over again *while he or she is sober* that you will no longer permit yourself to be abused. The problem drinker may not believe you and may even laugh at the suggestion that you will secure a restraining order from the local police, or take other concrete steps to prevent your being physically abused. In a way, you may not believe *yourself* as you issue this message. Only by resolving to take these steps, though, will you teach yourself and your alcoholic that you are changing. *Every time* your alcoholic attempts to physically abuse you, *you* must take some kind of action to prevent the abuse, even if it means going to the police or absenting yourself from the situation.

Verbal abuse must be countered just as firmly. One sad aspect about being told you are inadequate, stupid or worthless over an extended period of time is that you may begin to believe these negative messages. It is crazy to choose to be told such things by someone who is drunk. Advise your problem drinker in the strongest possible terms, while he or she is sober, that you will not tolerate being called names anymore. The next time it happens, immediately extract yourself from the situation, leave the room, go for a walk or take in a movie with a friend or by yourself.

3. *Begin a life outside your relationship with your problem drinker.* Start to do things for yourself *outside* your relationship with the problem drinker. You must break out of the isolation the other person's drinking problem has created for you. If you have become progressively more

encapsulated in that relationship, then chances are you now experience almost constant feelings of depression and loneliness and a sense of a lack of personal worth. In order to "get better," you must begin to get involved with activities beyond those of your alcoholic family system. To feel better, to do interesting things, to have more fun—to change in spite of your choice to continue living with a problem drinker—you must begin to structure your life differently. If your problem drinker refuses to go out to dinner or to a play or movie, party, meeting or lecture, then you must make arrangements to go by yourself or with friends. If your problem drinker is unwilling to plan a weekend trip or vacation with you, then plan your own holiday. Don't permit yourself to be alone unwillingly within the confines of your relationship with the problem drinker. Do things for yourself and, if necessary, by yourself.

4. *Find and nurture* new *relationships*. I am firmly convinced that at some point in every intimate relationship with a problem drinker it becomes virtually impossible for the parties involved to grow and change adaptively through their own relationship. So, related to step three is the requirement that you begin to develop *new relationships*. This step is difficult as it

requires you to initiate things. You must meet and acquaint yourself with new people. You will probably also have to reassess your connections with old friends, relatives and acquaintances. At first, you may feel uneasy or socially inept in your attempts to become meaningfully involved with other people. You will probably think that other people want little, if anything, to do with you. But if you are willing to take the initial steps necessary to create personal change, eventually you will discover that other people can contribute greatly to your personal growth and development. Such groups as Al-Anon and Alateen may be excellent starting points in your search for new friends who are willing to share their strengths, insights and compassion. I have found the people in these organizations to be empathic, accepting, supportive and relationship-oriented.

Personal change never occurs in a vacuum, but only in the context of relationships with other people. You may have been changing within the context of your relationship with your problem drinker for a long time, but not for the better. This is not really the problem drinker's fault, for you have chosen to make yourself unhappy and depressed by choosing to accept the bounds and limits of that destructive relationship. The responsibility for changing is yours, but you will find that it is easier to change through the love and concern of others.

At this point I'd like to recommend that you at least consider changing through a relationship with a professional counselor or therapist. Because I am a clinical psychologist I am naturally biased, but I have seen numerous loved ones of problem drinkers change and grow in many positive directions as a result of choosing to involve themselves in a psychotherapeutic relationship. After all, such relationships are first and foremost human relationships! Even if you feel strongly that you are not in need of "treatment," I still urge you to consider the psychotherapy alternative. You need to establish an open, honest, trusting, self-disclosing form of relationship with at least one other human being at this time, and a therapist is one person who should be capable of helping you do so.

One word of caution. Don't get out of your relationship with a problem drinker and then involve yourself in an intimate relationship with another problem drinker. This pattern occurs frequently within the context of marriage. Some women are married and divorced to as many as five or six problem drinkers. This pattern is related to the type of people you choose to involve yourself with and where you meet them. Bars, night clubs and taverns are generally poor places to establish new and meaningful relationships.

5. *Shape up physically.* Constructive change must include attention to your physical health and well-being. Living with a problem drinker causes a good deal of emotional stress and strain which typically results in a chronic sense of physical exhaustion and a lot of bad health habits. Nearly all of my patients who were living with a problem drinker when they started therapy were in very poor physical condition.

How long has it been since you looked at yourself in a full-length mirror? How do you feel about the *physical* person you see there? Do you look tired, run down, depressed or exhausted? And what about the clothes you are wearing? Do they enhance or hurt your physical image?

Taking care of yourself physically means a number of things. Stress, anxiety, depression, anger and other emotional factors can directly affect eating habits, so dieting is often crucial to the would-be survivor of a problem drinker. Overeating, eating inappropriate foods or not being able to eat at all are problems commonly found in those close to alcoholics.

Exercise is also essential to developing a

physical sense of well-being. You need to get in shape in order to begin to feel better emotionally. Take up yoga, learn a new sport like golf or tennis or go for jogs or walks for twenty or thirty minutes a day. The process of positive change is made easier when we involve our physical being. By changing our physical appearance and physical sense of self, we can help to change our feelings and thoughts.

Physical change for you might also involve eliminating or significantly reducing any addiction to caffeine, sugar or nicotine. Drinking ten or fifteen cups of coffee daily, munching on sweets all day, or chain-smoking are all habits born of tension and anxiety and obviously bad for your health and well-being.

Let me emphasize that changing your physical condition requires a *long-term* commitment. How many people have you known who were on a diet one week and literally eating like a hog the next? This is in fact the problem drinker's pattern—swearing "never to touch the stuff again" for a day or month, and then drunk again. Jogging daily for a week or a couple of months is not enough. Losing ten pounds and then gaining it all back in a week or a month is not enough. Tending to your personal grooming for a few days is not enough.

Taking the step toward better physical health and fitness must be a permanent commitment.

6. *Change yourself on a daily basis.* This brings us to the sixth and most important ingredient in the process of changing yourself. You must work at *each* of the five steps I have discussed *each day, one day at a time.* Changing yourself can begin by practicing only one or two of the steps on a daily basis, but eventually "working" only one or two of the steps will not be enough. You will need to change and grow into all of the steps; you can't expect to change overnight. Likewise, it is unrealistic to expect to implement all of the steps every day, particularly during the initial weeks of your change process. Start with step one and, as you begin to feel that you are consistently interacting with your problem drinker in accord with this step, move along to the second step, and so on until you have worked through step five. Do not anticipate being able to practice each step with equal success every time you try. Expect relapses and setbacks. Remember, as you change, your problem drinker is likely to become angry, accusing and even more manipulative. Your problem drinker *does not want you to change,* and will become the biggest single obstacle to

changing yourself if you choose to let that happen.

Also be aware that the change process, particularly as it occurs in the framework of outside relationships, may provoke guilt feelings in you. Remember that positive change and creative growth through a relationship with a drinking alcoholic is impossible. Your changing is needed, appropriate and not a rational basis for feeling guilty.

Above all, step number six means working at living in the present. Your problem drinker lives in the past and the future, not the present. The longer you have shared life with a problem drinker, the more you have probably lived in the past. By being preoccupied with past hurts, feelings and experiences, you have made yourself miserable in the here-and-now, and indeed you are no longer able to live effectively in the present. But your commitment to working these six steps will help you begin to center your life in the present. You cannot "undo" the past, or go back and re-live your life. You cannot wait for tomorrow, next week or next year to live your life, either. If you want to change your life and your life-style for the better, begin the process today.

Steps Toward Helping
the Problem Drinker Change

Your relationship with a problem drinker can become a potent vehicle of change for that person. But for this to happen, you must consistently behave differently within the context of that relationship.

This will not always be easy. Your positive growth, the result of working the steps we discussed earlier, will at first confuse the problem drinker. The signs of change in your life will encourage the problem drinker to further demonstrate his or her alcoholic character traits.

That person will consciously and unconsciously try to make it harder for you to change. After the initial resistance that the alcoholic displays toward your changing, you can expect to encounter less conflict, but as long as the alcoholic continues to drink and in other ways resist change, you will remain the target of feelings of resentment, anger and jealousy.

Your strategy at this point should be organized around three general approaches to the problem: (1) detachment, (2) selective confrontation and (3) timely assistance in helping the problem drinker seek outside help. Let's look at these approaches more closely.

DETACHMENT.

You need to begin to *detach* yourself from the irresponsible and irrational behaviors of the problem drinker. This issue was touched on in the previous chapter. Detachment does not mean that you have quit loving and caring for the problem drinker, although this person will probably interpret your detachment to mean that, and resent you for it. But unless you detach yourself, the drinker will not experience the logical and natural consequences of his or her alcoholic behavior. These consequences are unpleasant and even painful, but more than anything else, they often "push" a drinker into sobriety and behavioral change. So you must allow the problem drinker to fully experience the negative consequences of his or her drinking behavior if you are to help that person change. This sounds cold and lacking in compassion, but whenever you eliminate the pain associated with the problem, you actually reinforce further drinking and other unacceptable behaviors. And don't ever put yourself in a position which results in *your* having to experience pain for the drinker.

Healthy detachment also means avoiding attempts to inflict pain on the problem drinker, as so many people do who have lived with an alcoholic for extended periods. The verbal or physical pain which you can inflict upon the drinker won't make his or her alcoholism go away. When you attempt to punish or "get even" with your problem drinker, it is you and not the problem drinker that usually ends up feeling upset and remorseful. You cannot be a constructive instrument of change in the relationship as long as you are driven by feelings of resentment, anger and hostility.

Detachment can be psychological or physical.

When you are able to stop allowing your problem drinker to upset you, that person is no longer in control of your life. This is one form of psychological detachment. Physical detachment may mean leaving the room, moving out of the house or terminating sexual intimacy. All of these strategies place the problem drinker in a better position to experience the consequences of his or her irrational drinking behavior.

As you become emotionally stronger, your problem drinker will begin to behave differently. As noted earlier, you can anticipate that the problem drinker will initially be confused, angry and resentful toward you. That's o.k.! Just continue to detach yourself from the problem drinker and allow that person to be as angry, upset and confused as he or she wants to be. Remember, it's the problem drinker who has the problem, not you! Your problem drinker will resent your growth and healthy changes and double the effort to encapsulate you in the emotional turmoil of drinking. One spouse of a problem drinker who entered therapy reported that as she was better able to detach herself from her addicted spouse, through an active involvement in Al-Anon, she was continuously accused of being homosexual by the problem drinker.

Many problem drinkers begin to drink more unless their loved ones gain the strength and ability to "detach themselves with love." Most commonly, this stage is rather shortlived and the problem drinker, as a result of being painfully confronted with the reality of his or her drinking behavior, begins to evidence positive changes. One adolescent problem drinker, after terminating her drinking behavior, told her parents she couldn't stand the aloofness and detachment which they began to show toward her after they entered therapy. According to this patient, drinking became less important when her parents stopped reacting emotionally to her intoxication.

CONFRONTATION.

It is vital, in order to move your relationship off center, to begin to *confront* the problem drinker with your feelings and perceptions about his or her drinking and related irrational behavior. Never do this when the alcoholic is actually intoxicated, however. The best therapy in the world is a complete waste of time when conducted with a drunk! It may be difficult to restrain yourself the first few times you decide not to *react* to the problem drinker after the drinking has started. Secretly, the problem drinker has been using your emotional and verbal reactions to his or her drinking as a means for rationalizing further intoxication. In fact, this way the problem drinker can blame you for the whole problem.

The best time to confront the problem drinker is when that person has not been drinking and is willing to listen to you. The "morning after" or any other time when the alcoholic is in the process of sobering up may be selected for confrontation. But in order to help your problem drinker change, you must be able to consistently confront your problem drinker *in a healthy way* about the many destructive realities surrounding his or her addictive behaviors.

No single approach or style of confrontation is right for every relationship. If you try crying, screaming, whining and other emotional displays, you only defeat your own purpose. Effective confrontation requires a rational approach which emphasizes facts, specifics and actual behavior. If you can point out things that happen when the problem drinker is drinking, and how you feel about them, without becoming emotionally out of control, the confrontation will find its mark.

All too often people who live with an alcoholic fail to make that person fully aware of the reality of his or her addiction. Such a stance is just as destructive as constant and indiscriminate confrontation with a problem drinker. Both extremes tend to reinforce further intoxication.

If you choose not to confront and not to intervene, you really are choosing to let the problem drinker suffer needlessly, perhaps even to die. Spouses of drinkers are not the only ones guilty of this. Supervisors and managers are often afraid to confront an alcoholic employee, even though alcoholism clearly results in poor work performance, absenteeism and difficulties with co-workers. Therapists who "miss" the addiction of their patients, and choose to focus upon other symptoms, also actively contribute to the deterioration of the people they are supposed to be helping.

Whenever you confront your problem drinker, expect responses which serve the purpose of avoiding and denying the issue of alcoholism. Even your most rational, timely and supportive confrontations will initially precipitate feelings of anger, resentment, denial and disinterest upon the part of the problem drinker. In spite of these difficulties, you must remain consistent and untiring in your calm showdowns with the problem drinker. Eventually, you will discover that the problem drinker is listening to your confrontations. Confrontation represents a method of communication which says, "I still care." When you give up and no longer care, you will stop confronting the problem drinker.

TIMELY ASSISTANCE.

Eventually, it is to be hoped that your personal growth, along with your practice of these strategies of detachment and confrontation, will result in a desire on the part of the problem drinker to do something constructive about his or her drinking. Even the simple acknowledgment by this person that he or she "has a problem" with alcohol can be a turning point in the history of the problem and your relationship. It is true that "talk is cheap," but the verbal expression of a wish to live differently is often an important first step in the process of change. Whenever the drinker states, "I have a problem with alcohol" or "I'm an alcoholic," you should listen, show concern and reinforce this self-evaluation. The problem drinker must never be discounted when expressing concern about being addicted to alcohol or "drinking too damn much"—even if the problem drinker has expressed these concerns many times before and subsequently failed to make a commitment to sobriety.

When the problem drinker shows a desire to quit drinking and live more rationally, you should express your willingness to actively participate in whatever form of treatment he or she decides to become involved in. When the problem drinker tells you he or she is ready for help, make every effort to get help *at that time*. Do not wait until tomorrow to call your local alcoholic treatment center, community mental health center, Alcoholics Anonymous or the other sources of help discussed in the last chapter.

Frequently, people who have been living with alcoholics are extremely reluctant to involve themselves in any kind of treatment or rehabilitation program which will require *them* to share the problem, the treatment process and eventually to accept some degree of responsibility for the recovery process. It is true that the alcoholic has the problem and, as such, must be responsible for changing his or her addictive pattern of living. However, living with a problem drinker constitutes a very real problem for all involved in such relationships. Most alcoholics are afraid to commit themselves to a rehabilitation program. By choosing to involve yourself in the initial step of seeking treatment *with* your problem drinker, you may be taking an important step in the process of constructing a new and healthier relationship with your problem drinker.

However, entering treatment with the drinker should also represent a desire upon your part to help *yourself*. The help that the problem drinker receives as a result of your decision to be involved in the treatment is frosting on the cake. If you have decided to be involved in treatment solely for the sake of the problem drinker, you may be attempting to control the drinker. At some point, he or she will begin to resent and resist your reform efforts. When only one family member or marital partner is committed to the treatment process, conflicts tend to continue and divorce more frequently occurs. But when each family member makes a personal commitment to the treatment process, all involved are more likely to show positive growth and change. If you have rejected treatment for yourself, chances are good that living with a sober problem drinker will continue to be very difficult.

People who live with a drinking alcoholic tend to believe that the only problem they have is the drinking problem. This is simply not true. Many problems are associated with the prolonged experience of living with an alcoholic, and these various problems must be faced and managed after the addicted family member enters treatment and is able to establish sobriety. The real work of living together more rationally and adaptively begins *after* the addicted family member is able to quit drinking.

Learning New Ways
to Communicate with and
Relate to the Problem Drinker

The ultimate key to changing a relationship with a problem drinker is in the hands of the problem drinker, *not you*. The matter of drinking alcoholically is at the heart of the problem, and only through sobriety can a relationship change substantially. Significant improvements in a relationship can only take place after the drinker terminates his or her addiction. With this reality in mind, you may be confronted with a dilemma. You cannot control or change the drinking behavior of the problem drinker. Yet, *you* are capable of behaving differently within the context of your relationship with your problem drinker, and this means that you can effect or cause positive change in your relationship with your problem drinker. I will begin the discussion of how to change your relationship with your problem drinker with a number of general points.

Your relationship with the problem drinker can change radically if you begin to *communicate* more effectively. Most of the couples and families I have worked with in therapy were not even capable of talking to each other as human beings when they first entered treatment. It is, of course, impossible to communicate effectively with any person who is intoxicated. So a basic ground rule which you must begin to follow is that of *not* becoming caught up in the communication pattern your problem drinker adopts when drinking.

The "not talking" pattern of communication is also extremely damaging to any relationship. At the core of this pattern is a great deal of mutual anger. It is hard to talk *with*, not to or at, the people that we are angry with. Communication of whatever variety is dehumanizing when steeped in anger. None of us likes to be called names or blamed for things. Do you from time to time (or perhaps continuously) belittle your problem drinker? Do you blame him or her for financial problems, your bad nerves or your child's poor school performance? Messages of this kind tell the problem drinker to continue drinking. The drinker construes such messages as a kind of permission from you to keep on drinking. Remember, most alcoholics have been down on themselves all their lives. They've been on the receiving end of negative messages. By continuing this pattern, you make it harder for the problem drinker to choose to give up the addiction.

One couple I worked with in therapy avoided any form of verbal communication for weeks at a time following arguments or "blowups" centered around the husband's drinking behavior. Secretly, both spouses fantasized about killing each other throughout these periods of silence. This is a clear example of the angry and destructive effect of not talking which occurs in marital and family relationships involving a problem drinker. Try to keep your "channel" open.

Talk to the drinker as an equal. It is important for you to be aware of the fact that, as you have lost respect for your problem drinker over the months or years and have learned not to trust and believe in that person, you have come to think of the drinker as someone on a level beneath you. Without realizing it, you have taught yourself to talk down to the problem drinker.

You may not savor the idea of equality with a problem drinker, but now you must try to communicate a sense of respect and dignity for that person whenever you can. Don't try once or twice and give up. Rather, learn to consistently address the person in a tone and manner befitting an equal, so that you communicate a basic sense of dignity, worth and respect for that person.

Perhaps you are saying to yourself, "All of this sounds well and good, but *my* drinker is the type of person who is always belittling and verbally attacking me. How can *I* be expected to show concern, respect and dignity for such a person?" The answer is to relate to *yourself* in a manner which conveys a sense of your own worth and dignity. This will force you to quit tolerating verbal abuse from the drinker. Your style of communicating together will only start changing after you *demand* to be treated with dignity, respect and love. If you begin to interact in a manner which conveys to the drinker that he or she is, in fact, human and lovable, you will find the courage and strength to demand similar treatment in return. It will become progressively easier for the drinker to relate to you as a friend and equal.

Set aside time each week for two thirty-minute meetings specifically devoted to relating and communicating. These meetings should be held in a quiet room. They should be open-ended— with no limit in terms of topics of conversation. The emotional atmosphere should be nonjudgmental. Simply learning how to talk to each other again is a major goal of all concerned in a relationship involving a problem drinker.

Communicate in the here-and-now. Talk about *present* feelings and issues. Your relationship has been steeped in hurt, resentment, anger and similar negative feelings and experiences. If you dredge up this material from the past, you can only expect angry, hostile and ineffective communications and interactions to persist. But make no mistake about this: it can be very difficult to learn to live, relate and communicate without reference to the past of a troubled relationship. That is why, if this is a hurdle you and your problem drinker can't seem to overcome in spite of your best efforts, it is advisable to seek outside help in the form of family or marital therapy.

Many couples and families discover that they are unable to escape the past of their relationships, even after the problem drinker has stopped drinking. Their patterns of communication and relating continue to be ineffective and disturbed. One family entered therapy for these very reasons. The parents and two sons seemed obsessed about the former sexual promiscuity of an adolescent girl in the family. The daughter had totally abstained from alcohol for some ten months, and she had ceased all promiscuous behavior. In spite of these healthy changes, the family could not stop bringing up the daughter's past.

Beyond communicating more effectively, one of the most important single ways to initiate constructive relationship change is to learn how to do things together again. As simple as this may sound, I have found in my practice that doing things together is a difficult, if not initially impossible, prescription to follow for couples and families with an alcohol problem. It is as uncomfortable for the nonaddicted spouse, children and other family members to begin to share the experience of living together as it is for the drinker. People find the alcoholic difficult to be around after sobriety is attained because in some ways that person is a new and very different person.

Going for walks, out to eat or on a vacation may or may not have been things you did together when the problem drinker was drinking. In any case, engaging in these activities with a sober alcoholic is a different matter, and all parties involved have to learn, and unlearn, how to cope with it in order to begin to interact more effectively.

You must decide to put forth the effort required to do new and different things, and to take the risk of behaving differently together. Your relationship can only change as a result of mutual learning experiences. To decide to unlearn the neurotic roles and patterns in your past together is to expect new and more adaptive relationship behavior to occur in the present and the future.

Ultimately, the troubled partners must develop a capacity for *intimate* relating and communicating. This transcends merely doing things together and talking to each other, and is especially difficult for the person who has been consistently and deeply hurt. Bear in mind that many problem drinkers believe they do not deserve to be loved, and chose to drink in the first place because they lacked positive feelings of self-worth. Nevertheless, if your relationship with the problem drinker has progressed to the stage of sobriety, and you are talking and communicating more effectively, and behaving and interacting more adaptively, both or all of you are ready to begin working at intimate living and loving. This requires mutual trust, honesty and openness.

Sharing feelings, experiences and thoughts in an intimate fashion can be difficult. Intimate sexuality includes mutual loving, caring and concern. Just as caring sexual experiences transcend mere performance, intimate patterns of relating and communicating go beyond merely talking and doing things together.

Let me now summarize, in the form of "do's" and "don't's," the various steps and strategies I have advocated for living more effectively in any relationship with a problem drinker. These steps apply whether the person you are living with is still drinking or is in the process of treatment and recovery—and even if that person has been sober for months or years! Remember, the more persistently and consistently you follow these guidelines, the sooner your relationship will begin to change and grow constructively.

Guidelines for Building a New Relationship with a Problem Drinker

Do's	Don't's
1. Do take care of yourself physically, psychologically and spiritually.	1. Don't permit yourself to be abused, physically or psychologically.
2. Do take care of your children (if this applies to your situation).	2. Don't give up your spirituality.
3. Do ask for help.	3. Don't permit and tolerate the drinking behavior of the problem drinker.
4. Initiate therapy for yourself or self-help.	4. Don't attempt to cover up for the problem drinker.
5. Do continue to live responsibly.	5. Don't blame, threaten, nag or complain.
6. Do continue to love yourself and the problem drinker.	6. Don't hide the liquor or pour it down the drain.
7. Do continue to attempt to understand yourself and your relationship dilemmas.	7. Don't drink with the problem drinker as a solution to relationship conflicts.
8. Do continue to work at the total process of changing yourself.	8. Don't try to change or control the problem drinker.
9. Do enter treatment *with* the problem drinker when he or she takes that first step.	9. Don't expect the problem drinker to quit tomorrow or change overnight.
10. Do begin to work on each of these "do's" *today*.	10. Don't give up—on yourself, the problem drinker or your relationship.

11. By *doing* today, do expect to personally grow and change tomorrow!

11. Don't attempt to live with the anger, rage, resentment and other emotional conflicts caused by the alcoholic relationship.
12. Don't be afraid to ask for help for yourself, or to *demand* help for the problem drinker.
13. Don't ever forget that you have chosen to live with the problem drinker and that other alternatives are available to you.
14. Don't expect your relationship to grow, develop and mature if the problem drinker won't actively commit himself or herself to some form of ongoing treatment program.
15. Don't wait until tomorrow to begin behaving and living differently and more rationally within the context of your relationship with the problem drinker.

Surviving with the Sober Problem Drinker

Living with a sober or "recovered" problem drinker can be for better or worse. It is, at least in certain respects, almost always easier to live with a sober problem drinker than with a *drinking* problem drinker. But living happily with a sober problem drinker poses its own special problems.

The period of the first few weeks and months of sobriety is usually the most difficult for everyone involved in this situation. Everyone involved with a "recovering" problem drinker must work with sobriety on a day-by-day basis. Some problem drinkers find the first few weeks of sobriety a breeze, so easy that they decide to get drunk again, in the false belief that it is easy for them to quit and that they can quit any time they decide to do so. In truth, the vast majority of people who are alcoholic or who have a serious drinking problem are not able to remain abstinent after they have entered a treatment program, or Alcoholics Anonymous, or after having committed themselves to some other program which they feel will help them remain sober.

A sense of futility can be expected to follow the first "slip." This sense of futility includes other sentiments and feelings as well. After a relapse, the problem drinker, as well as everyone living with the problem drinker, may consciously feel depressed, angry and radiate a "to hell with it" attitude.

If your problem drinker has recently decided to "do something about his or her drinking," meaning a commitment to some form of rehabilitation, psychotherapy or Alcoholics Anonymous, it is equally unrealistic for *you* to expect the drinking problem to be over or solved. It is statistically absurd for you or your problem drinker to believe after initially entering treatment that he or she "will never drink again."

This is in many ways a good attitude to enter treatment or therapy with, but experience indicates that such an expectancy is highly unrealistic.

Whether or not the problem drinker will remain sober is, of course, the main issue during this time and the one which provokes the most tension. If an alcoholic has been sober for five, ten or twenty-five years, his or her sobriety is not nearly so tenuous. Such a person can be confidently relied upon to continue to be sober, although there are noteworthy exceptions to this as well.

In my own work, I have consistently found that the individual who is able to remain totally abstinent for at least seven or eight months, while at the same time being committed to some form of psychotherapy and participation in Alcoholics Anonymous, has an excellent chance to remain sober. Such individuals generally begin to function much better in many other areas of living as well, and long-term sobriety usually correlates with more rational thinking, better decision-making, improved judgment, improved relationships, a higher frustration tolerance and an overall improvement in psychological and physical status.

In spite of this optimistic picture, too many

people expect too much too soon. The problem
drinker expects that all of his or her problems
will be solved with the attainment of sobriety.
Likewise, the spouse, children, relatives and
friends sometimes believe that "everything will
be o.k." once the problem drinker quits drinking.

Expecting too much too soon can actually
make it easier for the problem drinker to choose
to drink again. He or she may feel so let down
as a result of the new conflicts brought about
by sobriety that drinking again seems the best
way out. After a few days or weeks of sobriety,
many alcoholic persons find themselves feeling
agitated and upset, depressed, tense, unable to
sleep or eat well, preoccupied and unable to
think clearly. This general pattern of emotional
disturbance can persist for a number of months.
In some cases it persists for years in spite of
abstinence. In any event, there is much of an
unpleasant and uncertain nature in the first
prolonged period of sobriety.

At this point in the recovery process, you
must communicate to the problem drinker that
you don't expect a miraculous, overnight change.
Let the problem drinker know that you are
happy with his or her sobriety. Give the problem
drinker credit for the other changes that you
recognize. Remind yourself that change is usu-

ally slow and involves taking one step at a time. Help the problem drinker accept and appreciate the healthy changes he or she has initiated. Recognize the other changes that are needed and maintain an attitude of willingness to work with the problem drinker on facilitating change in other areas of living.

Don't expect the problem drinker to be at the apex of physical and emotional health immediately after sobering up. If the problem drinker feels he or she has failed you in this regard, chances are he will feel that once again he has failed himself, and possibly again turn to the bottle. If you let the problem drinker know you don't expect overnight miracles as a result of his or her sobriety, you help get the message across to that person not to expect too much too soon. Problem drinkers tend to be impulsive, perfectionistic people; they expect things to happen immediately, and this is a major psychological liability with which they must come to grips and change if they are to remain sober. By not falling into the trap of expecting the problem drinker to be a new person immediately after sobriety, you can help the person accept the necessarily slow process of growing, developing and changing. A day-by-day, one-step-at-a-time orientation toward life is essential for you and the problem drinker to circumvent the many pitfalls of this period of time.

Much of the anxiety, depression, resentment, anger and confusion which accompanies sobriety can be associated with the process of self-discovery. Your alcoholic has chosen, on thousands of occasions, to drink in order to avoid self-awareness. Your problem drinker has been dreadfully afraid of himself or herself for years. Your problem drinker is a person who fears his or her thoughts, feelings, fantasies and behaviors. Chronologically he may be forty-five or fifty years old when he finally sobers up, but in some ways, he is more like a fifteen-year-old. Chronic alcoholism always results in a serious social and psychological developmental lag. Sobering up results in a confrontation with the real self and with the past. As your problem drinker begins to experience raw feelings and emotions, and becomes increasingly aware of his or her many irrational behaviors, he or she will necessarily become a difficult person to live with. In order to grow psychologically, your problem drinker must suffer through the pain and turmoil of finding and discovering who he or she is. If the process of self-discovery is too emotionally threatening, he or she will choose to return to the more reliable form of self-avoidance and escape—intoxication.

You may find that *you* don't know what to do regarding the matter of drinking at parties or while entertaining. You may feel uncomfortable about having a drink or two when you know that the problem drinker is struggling with a commitment to sobriety. In situations such as this, it is important for you to remember who has the drinking problem. Assuming that you are not a problem drinker, it is generally all right to have a drink or two at social outings. In other cases, your decision to abstain may be helpful to the problem drinker.

The newly sober problem drinker has a hard time facing up to his or her past life-style and all the behaviors which were so distorted as a result of alcoholism. I have seen problem drinkers actually become nauseous in trying to verbalize previous alcohol-facilitated escapades. This particular situation is generally limited to the first few months of sobriety.

People close to the problem drinker sometimes decide that early in the process of sobriety is a good time to get even with the problem drinker for all the pain and difficulty he or she has inflicted upon them. People realize, consciously or unconsciously, that the problem drinker is now extremely vulnerable. In the past, while intoxicated, the problem drinker did not fully hear and feel the statements of confrontation that came from those closest to him. With sobriety the alcoholic hears and feels everything. Obviously, this is not the time to make your point about past behavior if you honestly want to help the problem drinker stay sober. It is not necessary to walk on eggs conversationally with the problem drinker at this time, but it is important to avoid making it easier for the problem drinker to choose further intoxication as a result of your anger, hostility and resentment.

A particular sore spot at this time for some problem drinkers is the topic of sex. Don't confront and bombard the newly sober problem drinker with a detailed history of his or her sexual problems, promiscuity or deviations. Remember, the sexual difficulties of the problem drinker usually become more manageable or are no longer problems after sobriety occurs. This may take some time. If you are married to a problem drinker, your sex life should improve with sobriety. Should you or your problem drinker encounter persistent serious sexual problems such as impotence, frigidity and premature ejaculation after the problem drinker has been abstinent for a number of months, it would be wise to seek out professional treatment in this area.

Start allowing the problem drinker to be responsible for his or her behavior as soon as sobriety has been established. Until this point in time, the problem drinker probably has found it difficult to live responsibly, and the burden of paying bills, arranging family matters, and so on, has fallen on you. Now the problem drinker needs to learn how to perform the duties that are properly his or her own. By learning to live responsibly, the problem drinker will begin to respect himself or herself more and become free to show more love and respect for you.

Rather commonly, the problem drinker who has just sobered up will demand all the various responsibilities which he or she has avoided and neglected during the years of drinking. You must be willing to discuss this issue carefully with the problem drinker at this time in order to find a way to fairly share jobs and duties. There's a danger in dumping everything on the shoulders of the newly sober drinker, because in this period of adjustment he or she really is not ready for it.

After the initial seven or eight months of

sobriety, living with a sober problem drinker should become progressively easier and more rewarding. With prolonged sobriety, the problem drinker becomes less uptight and anxious, less angry, less depressed and psychologically more integrated. Many of the families that I have worked with in therapy have reported that after eighteen or twenty months of sobriety, the alcoholic involved became *radically* easier to live with.

Total abstinence is absolutely necessary for this happy result to come about. Alcoholics who play with sobriety—who remain sober for a few days or months at a time only to return to drinking—continue to be seriously impaired psychologically, and so do not become much easier to live with. In fact, these problem drinkers tend to operate on an emotional roller coaster, and those who live with them are usually taken on that same ride.

After attaining a period of relatively stable sobriety, the problem drinker is faced with the tasks of living rationally and effectively while sober. Very few alcoholic persons can successfully negotiate this process on their own, which is why some organized form of long-term recovery program is essential. There are no guarantees on this matter, but I have found that mutual commitments to recovery foster greater relationship change and happiness. This means joint participation in rehabilitation and therapy, Alcoholics Anonymous and Al-Anon, church programs or other treatment programs.

Here, in a nutshell, are some guidelines for a rational and successful life with a sober problem drinker:

(1) Live with patience through the initial weeks and months of sobriety with your problem drinker. In many ways, this will be a most difficult and trying time for you and the problem drinker.

(2) Remember that *you* must learn to live rationally and differently than before with your sober problem drinker. Sobriety means discovering who *you* are, who your problem drinker is, and what your relationship is all about.

(3) Don't expect too much too soon.

(4) You have the right to expect your relationship with your problem drinker to improve following sobriety as long as *you* are committed to changing and improving your relationship.

(5) Both of you (or all of you, meaning everybody involved in the relationship with the

problem drinker) need to commit yourselves to some or all of the "do's" and "don't's" discussed in the previous chapter *as soon as your problem drinker becomes sober,* if not earlier.

(6) Don't forget that the problem drinker has the challenging task of finding, through sobriety and recovery, how to live with himself or herself more rationally in order to live more rationally and adaptively with you.

(7) Sobriety alone is never enough! Your life with the problem drinker will become more rewarding and pleasant only if personal and relationship growth and change take place at the same time. The change process is a life-long endeavor. Even if your problem drinker has been sober for twenty years, all of you must continue to grow and change.

Surviving without the
Problem Drinker

If your relationship with the problem drinker
is totally unrewarding and negative, it is altogether proper for you to choose to end this
relationship. This applies to relationships with
the sober problem drinker as well as with the
drinking alcoholic.

Living with a sober problem drinker will not
make life easier and more rewarding for you
if you are *living alone in the relationship*. If
your relationship is no better than it was when
your loved one was drinking, sobriety by itself

means little if anything. If the problem drinker continues to be depressed, hostile, nervous and self-centered after two or three years of sobriety, the overall quality of your relationship will have changed very little. If *you* are still upset, resentful, depressed and generally unhappy, what have you gained?

When does the relationship really come to a dead end? I think this happens when you give up all *hope* for relationship growth and improvement, after having worked hard at the processes of changing yourself and your relationship for at least eighteen months to two years. It is important to have committed yourself to the process of relationship change for a good length of time prior to deciding to end your relationship with the problem drinker. This means an extended commitment to some form of therapy or rehabilitation. Such personal growth and behavioral change-inducing programs can prepare you for the process of terminating the relationship if this is to eventually occur.

Some people give up hope for relationship growth and change within a few weeks or months after the problem drinker becomes abstinent. This is too soon to give up on yourself and your relationship with the problem drinker.

Recovery takes time and a lot of mutual hard work. People who give up in a few weeks or months often miss the real rewards of the recovery process, and fail to experience the joy of positive relationship change and growth.

Therapy and rehabilitation can also help you know when and how to go about carrying out your choice. It is not time to terminate the relationship until you have worked through and resolved your role and emotional being within the context of this relationship. Until you have at least partially resolved the various feelings and conflicts associated with the relationship, you are not psychologically ready to end it.

How do you go about severing your relationship with the problem drinker? Any long-term relationship is, of course, difficult to end. But if you have truly prepared yourself for the process via extended personal work and commitment in psychotherapy, a self-help group or any combination of the other treatments discussed earlier, you will know a great deal about how to go about it. These steps will enable *you* to rationally choose to terminate your relationship with the problem drinker.

A basic sense of personal adequacy, worth and strength is essential to the process. This comes about through healthy interpersonal relationships with people other than the problem drinker. By creating and developing positive self-esteem, you will spontaneously begin to sever your parasitic and pathological ties with the problem drinker. Relevant and meaningful interpersonal involvements will make you feel less "controlled" by the problem drinker. When you begin to feel that you are less controlled, you can experience the freedom essential to knowing how to get out of the relationship altogether.

These are some of the important processes that you need to work on today if you are to eventually terminate your relationship with the problem drinker. You must experience and re-experience healthy connections with people other than the problem drinker to generate personal strength and confidence. If you haven't established a number of healthy friendships, you will be unable to end your unhealthy relationship, or you will continuously be unable to "decide" about ending it.

One big reason people hesitate to end their relationships with problem drinkers is fear. The alcoholic uses fear as a control tactic in his or her relationships with others. You will become capable of terminating your relationship with your problem drinker when you are no longer controlled by the fear you have of that person. If your alcoholic father has always told you that "If you ever walk out that door, don't expect to ever live here again," you will need to overcome your fears associated with not being able to move back in, if you do choose to leave. The fear of not being able to return home, in this situation, has been utilized by the father in order to control his child's avoidance behavior.

Some alcoholic husbands use their paranoid thoughts to control their wives, and this is always accomplished through the medium of fear. One such man tried to keep his wife from attending church by accusing her of having an affair with the minister, and stated that if she continued to go to church, he would "rightfully" kill the minister. It is rational to fear such a person, but it is irrational to allow yourself to be controlled by your fears. In effect, it is irrational to choose to live with the irrationality of such a person! You may need to move out, call the police, inform your therapist or take other direct steps in order to break out of the pattern of allowing the problem drinker to control you through fear.

You will not be able to terminate your relationship if you yourself use fear, such as continually threatening to get a divorce or to leave home, to try to control the problem drinker. Struggles to set limits or establish conditions in your living arrangement with the problem drinker are signs that you still somehow believe you can control that person. So long as you remain involved in such transactions, you're not ready to work on the "how to do it" aspects of terminating the relationship.

In preparing your exit from the relationship, you must be ready to deal with and manage a wide variety of living-and-surviving problems. These include being able to financially support yourself and any children involved, handling a change in residence, finding a job and coping with being alone. Confronted with such problems, you may decide to put your decision off for a few weeks or months. Your insecurities about living on your own increase the odds against ever successfully terminating your relationship with the problem drinker.

In this regard I think it is important for me to tell you that you can and will survive without the problem drinker once you manage to decide upon this course of action. After all, even though we tend to be insecure and fearful about life, the vast majority of us do survive for sixty-five to eighty years. Life is always difficult and filled with anxiety-producing events, but it does go on. You can survive without the problem drinker!

If you do what you need to do today in order to sever your ties with the problem drinker, you will be ready to proceed with the actual task tomorrow. If you think in terms of "ending all of it today," chances are that you will be so overwhelmed with the enormity of this process that you will either put it off or give up completely. Terminating the relationship requires *time*.

There are no pat answers to the question of how or when to end a relationship with a problem drinker, but, in summary, the following points should be kept in mind if you are to engage in the process rationally.

1. You are entitled to choose *not* to continue living with the problem drinker.

2. You should choose to end the relationship only after you have given up all *hope* for constructive change.

3. You will be able to rationally terminate the relationship only after *you* have adequately prepared yourself for the undertaking.

4. Ending the relationship is a process which requires time, but only by beginning to end the relationship *today* will you ever successfully actualize the process.

5. You can survive without the problem drinker; in fact, this may be the only way for you to live!

What You Should Know about Professional and Self-Help Treatments for Problem Drinking

The decision to seek out treatment is a hard one for the problem drinker to make. It isn't any easier for the person who is living with a problem drinker. Any decision to enter treatment requires determination to follow through on that course of action.

Most behavioral scientists who specialize in the treatment of alcoholism tend to view this disorder as family-oriented. This simply means that everyone who is living with a problem drinker is believed to become emotionally disturbed as a result of the alcoholic's affect on the family's life-style. Therefore, it is realistic for you to expect to be involved in the treatment process if you are the spouse, parent or child of a problem drinker who enters a treatment program.

As touched upon earlier in this book, when a problem drinker verbalizes a desire to enter treatment, you should make every effort to get that person to a program as soon as possible. Where to look for a program? A good place to begin is in the Yellow Pages of your phone book. Check the following headings: Alcoholism, Alcoholic Treatment Centers, Rehabilitation Centers, Mental Health Centers, Social Service Agencies, Hospitals and Clinics, Alcoholics Anonymous and National Council on Alcoholism. It is also appropriate to look under the headings of Physicians, Psychologists and Social Workers. Some of these professionals specialize in the treatment of problem drinking and alcoholism.

PROFESSIONAL TREATMENT.

Professional treatment programs vary considerably. Inpatient and residential treatment programs provide intensive care for the problem drinker on a "live-in" basis. In some residential programs, the problem drinker resides in a hospital setting on a twenty-four-hour-a-day basis for as long as six or eight weeks. Halfway house settings provide "live-in" care during the evenings and weekends. Many of these programs are conducted on a monthly basis. Outpatient programs may involve weekly or twice-weekly individual, group or family therapy sessions. Outpatient care may extend over a period of several months.

Many alcoholics require medical care prior to placement in a halfway house or an outpatient therapy program. Medical detoxification may be indicated for the physically addicted alcoholic. Detoxification is usually completed in four to ten days. If your problem drinker has been a daily drinker for several months or years, short-term medical evaluation and care will usually be required during the initial stage of the recovery process.

The most basic forms of professional treatment for problem drinking are individual, group and family therapy. These varieties of therapy are conducted by both inpatient and outpatient treatment facilities. Individual therapy involves talking with a counselor or therapist once or twice a week for approximately one hour at a time. During these sessions the problem drinker and therapist discuss alternatives to drinking, the patient's past and present life experiences, feelings and thoughts, and essentially everything and anything that pertains to the patient. Group therapy sessions are usually held once a week for a time interval of ninety minutes to two hours. Eight to fifteen individuals with drinking problems share their experiences, feelings and relationship conflicts with each other and a group leader. Family therapy sessions involve the problem drinker, spouse, children and a family therapist. Family sessions are held weekly and last for an hour to an hour and a half. The primary focus of family therapy is the family relationship. Patterns of family interaction and communication are explored within the context of family therapy.

Conjoint therapy is another form of treatment which involves the problem drinker and spouse. The marital relationship is the point of focus and exploration in conjoint therapy.

Therapists and agencies which provide treatment for problem drinkers and alcoholics vary according to treatment goals, therapy orientation and style of treatment. For example, behavior therapists tend to rely upon conditioning, teaching and direct training techniques. Aversive therapy, utilized by some behavioral therapists in the treatment of problem drinkers, involves the use of chemical or electrical shock to condition and teach the patient not to drink. Relaxation therapy, hypnosis and assertiveness training are rather common treatment approaches used with problem drinkers.

Some therapies and treatments are insight-oriented. According to this approach, problem drinkers will terminate their destructive patterns of drinking when they become more aware of themselves and the unconscious factors that cause them to drink. Whatever the therapy type, reassurance, concern and empathy for the patient are basic to supportive treatment strategies.

Many therapists and treatment programs recommend that the problem drinker be placed on an Antabuse maintenance program. There are many misconceptions about Antabuse and the use of this drug as a treatment for alcohol abuse. It is important for you to be aware of these misconceptions if your problem drinker is contemplating taking Antabuse. First of all, Antabuse does not take away the urge to drink. It is simply a drug which will precipitate an extremely adverse physiological and psychological reaction when combined with alcohol. Having been told the consequences of alcohol consumption while taking Antabuse, the problem drinker will abstain from drinking. The alcoholic who ingests liquor after taking the drug will experience extreme nausea, vomiting, fall in blood pressure, extreme headache, blurred vision and breathing difficulties. Therefore, if your problem drinker wants to begin taking Antabuse, make sure that he or she completes a medical examination and is cleared by a physician to take this potentially life-threatening medication.

Antabuse is like an insurance policy for many problem drinkers. After taking the drug in the morning, many problem drinkers feel relieved. They are assured that they will not drink that day. Some alcoholics have taken Antabuse daily for more than thirty years with no side effects. While it is not magic, Antabuse has helped thousands of alcoholics recover.

If your problem drinker decides to enter a treatment center, local hospital, mental health center or see a private therapist, expect to pay for the treatment. The cost varies greatly, according to where your problem drinker receives help and who provides the services. Private outpatient psychotherapy may cost as much as

$75–100 an hour. However, many private therapists operate on a "sliding fee" scale. This means that you are charged according to your income and other indicators of your ability to pay for services. Thus a private therapist may only charge five to twenty dollars per hour. Most mental health centers providing comprehensive alcoholism services also operate on a "sliding fee" scale. Hospital inpatient care for alcoholics often costs $100–200 per day. Hospital programs vary in length of stay, but many are of a thirty- to sixty-day duration. Halfway house treatment centers also vary considerably with regard to service costs. Intensive care and detoxification can be very expensive.

If your problem drinker decides to enter treatment, you should check into the issue of rehabilitation costs prior to deciding upon a particular program. Although a few thousand dollars, or even a few hundred dollars, may seem like a great deal of money to spend for therapy or treatment, in the long run this cost may be very small. Commonly, problem drinkers spend hundreds and thousands of dollars each year drinking!

When looking into the matter of treatment costs, check also your family health insurance program. Employed problem drinkers usually have company insurance programs which pay for some portion, if not all, of their treatment expenses. Today, many of our bigger corporations provide for alcoholism treatment at no cost to the employee.

Finally, it is important for your problem drinker to enter treatment with a *qualified* therapist. If you and your problem drinker decide to enter therapy with a psychologist, psychiatrist, social worker or counselor, make sure that your therapist is experienced, trained and skilled in the explicit areas of alcoholism and problem drinking treatment. The fact that your therapist has an M.D., Ph.D., Ed.D. or whatever other degree or degrees is no guarantee of competence and expertise in the treatment of alcoholism.

While there are no absolute guarantees of skill in treating problem drinkers, you can begin by discussing this matter with your family physician and consulting recognized alcoholism experts in your community. Relatively few psychiatrists, psychologists and other professionally trained behavioral scientists are experienced, trained and skilled in the realm of treating problem drinkers.

SELF-HELP ALTERNATIVES.

Self-help is an alternative to professional help for the problem drinker. Alcoholics Anonymous and the AA community (Al-Anon, Alateen and Alatot) are by far the largest and most recognized effective self-help programs available for problem drinkers, with hundreds of thousands of people involved throughout the world. The only requirement for membership in Alcoholics Anonymous is a desire to stop drinking. Al-Anon is a self-help program primarily for the spouse of the alcoholic, but the parents, adult children and other loved ones of the alcoholic can also become involved. The only requirement for membership in Al-Anon is living with or having lived with a problem drinker. Alateen is a self-help program for the teenage children living in a family which includes a problem drinker. Alatot is a self-help program for the younger children living in a family which includes a problem drinker.

In the AA program there are no membership dues or fees for treatment. This self-help program is based upon anonymity. The AA, Al-Anon, Alateen and Alatot programs of recovery are based upon the following twelve steps.

We

(1) Admitted we were powerless over alcohol —that our lives had become unmanageable.

(2) Came to believe that a Power greater than ourselves could restore us to sanity.

(3) Made a decision to turn our will and lives over to the care of God as we understood Him.

(4) Made a searching and fearless moral inventory of ourselves.

(5) Admitted to God, to ourselves and to another human being the exact nature of our wrongs.

(6) Were entirely ready to have God remove all these defects of character.

(7) Humbly asked Him to remove our shortcomings.

(8) Made a list of all persons we had harmed and became willing to make amends to them all.

(9) Made direct amends to such people whenever possible, except when to do so would injure them or others.

(10) Continued to take personal inventory and when we were wrong promptly admitted it.

(11) Sought through prayer and meditation to improve our conscious contact with God as we understood Him, praying only for knowledge of His will for us and the power to carry that out.

(12) Having had a spiritual awakening as the result of these steps, tried to carry this message to alcoholics and to practice it in all our affairs.

Unlike professional treatment programs for problem drinking, the AA program is concrete, rather specific and comparatively simple. Today, Alcoholics Anonymous, Al-Anon and Alateen meetings are held in virtually every community in America. Meetings take place every night, weekends included, and frequently lunch-hour meetings are also available in larger communities. Professional counseling services are not provided by Alcoholics Anonymous. However, new members in AA and Al-Anon are encouraged to select a sponsor and work on personal and emotional problems with this person. The sponsor has usually been an active member of AA or Al-Anon for years. Sponsors who are AA members typically have been totally abstinent for several years. A major reason why many people choose to seek out help within the AA community rests with the fact that there are no fees for treatment in AA, Al-Anon, Alateen or Alatot. Along with this factor, you do not need to attend one of the meetings to get help. By simply calling a phone number you can talk to someone who has in all probability experienced the same difficulty you are struggling with.

If you decide to involve yourself in one of the AA programs of self-help, make a concentrated effort to benefit from the program. This means making an ongoing commitment to the self-help program of recovery with which you become involved. If you attend Al-Anon or Alateen only three or four times, it is unrealistic to expect to see yourself change and grow. In order to even understand any of the AA programs of recovery you will need to attend weekly or twice-weekly sessions for at least six months to one year. These programs are designed to help you and your problem drinker radically change your life-styles.

The Alcoholics Anonymous community is a spiritually oriented program of recovery. It is not a religious program per se, but rather incorporates the concept of "God as we understand Him." The spiritual aspects of AA are poorly understood by people who have not actively participated in the program. For this reason, some people believe that AA is for religious fanatics. Nothing is further from the truth.

OTHER SELF-HELP
ALTERNATIVES.

More and more problem drinkers are utilizing positive addictions in order to terminate their drinking behavior. Potentially, anyone who is living with a problem drinker can establish a positive addiction. A positive addiction involves specific ritualistic, almost compulsive patterns of behavior. A rather common positive addiction is jogging. The person who is positively addicted to jogging engages in this physical activity daily for a period of forty-five minutes to two hours. Seven days a week, regardless of temperature or weather, the individual can be found jogging at a particular time of the day. This behavior pattern must be continuous. When the addicted jogger is unable to maintain his or her daily running routine, anxiety, depression and irritability set in. When maintained, however, positive addictions help alleviate stress, anxiety, depression and anger. Other positive addictions include Transcendental Meditation, yoga, writing and needlepoint work.

Some people recover from alcoholism by establishing a religious affiliation. Although behavioral scientists have tended to be skeptical about this method of recovery, many individuals with drinking and emotional problems report being cured or helped following their involvement with a church or religiously-oriented group. Your local clergyman is a person you can turn to for emotional support and understanding. Many churches are beginning to provide direct counseling services for the problem drinker and other family members. People involved in any religious group are agents of change who can potentially provide you with self-help if you are living with a problem drinker.

There are many other self-help activities which you and your problem drinker can engage in as methods for enhancing psychological and physical strength. Dieting, exercising on a regular basis, developing new friends and new relationships, starting a hobby, taking vacations and otherwise enjoying your leisure time are but a few of the potentially meaningful self-help activities available to you and the problem drinker.

But it is vital for you to know when self-help is not enough. Problem drinking is a progressive disorder which eventually creates serious emotional, physical and relationship problems for everyone living with the alcoholic. After having committed yourself to the self-help alternatives discussed in this chapter for several months, attempt to objectively evaluate your behavior, thoughts and feelings. Get feedback from others. If you are still upset, depressed, angry, confused and your life is unmanageable, seek out professional treatment. Self-help in combination with professional treatment probably represents the most effective and efficient method for initiating as well as maintaining constructive change and growth.

Most people who enter treatment as a result of problem drinking are positively benefited. Some professional treatment programs report that eighty to ninety percent of their problem-drinking patients recover. Fifty percent of the people who enter AA get well in a short period of time. Another twenty-five percent take longer but eventually recover through the program. These general statistics also apply to the spouses and other loved ones of problem drinkers who enter professional treatment or self-help programs of recovery.

The people who continue to suffer and never recover are almost always those who reject and avoid treatment. If you are living with an alcoholic your problems will not magically go away. Your problem drinker will not simply quit drinking, nor will his or her emotional problems suddenly go away. In order to grow and change, you and your problem drinker need, more than anything else, to be involved in ongoing, healthy human relationships. You both need other people to recover!

DR. GARY G. FORREST, a licensed clinical psychologist in independent practice, is the Executive Director of Psychotherapy Associates, P.C. and The Institute for Addictive Behavioral Change in Colorado Springs, Colorado.

As an army officer in the 1970s, Dr. Forrest was the Clinical Director of Alcohol Rehabilitation at Fort Gordon, Georgia. He is an adjunct professor in the department of Psychology, Guidance and Counseling at the University of Northern Colorado.

Dr. Forrest lives with his wife, Sandra, and daughter, Sarah Ellen, in the Colorado Rocky Mountains. He is an avid sports enthusiast and enjoys skiing, jogging, writing and reading.